Jason,

May God Bless You as you discover and pursue his purpose in your life!

Prayerfully Yours,

Hab 2:2-3

# What's Your Purpose?

By

Timothy A. Carter

# Table of Contents

# Acknowledgment

**"Iron sharpeneth iron: so a man sharpeneth the countenance of his friend" Proverbs 27:17.**

In many ways I am a product of the observations I have made of several men GOD has placed into my life. These men have been an example of investing their lives with purpose. God has used these men to encourage me and provide me with valuable Godly counsel.

I want to thank my accountability partner for his encouragement and his prompting to write this book. I also wish to thank the men that provided me with such valuable input and critique while I was writing this book. Most of all, I wish to thank my best friend and partner in life, my precious wife. I praise God for you all and wish for you His greatest blessings!

# Introduction

I am often reminded of how our daily lives can quickly turn into years of repeated activities with little or no eternal impact. It is so easy to get caught up in our routines, and before we realize it, several years have passed and we find ourselves asking, "Why am I doing what I do?".

I wrote this book thinking that I was probably not alone in asking that same question. At 46 years old, I have spent a considerable part of my life developing what our society refers to as my "career". In reflecting back over this career building exercise, I began to think more about why I was doing what I did, rather than what I was doing. Was I pursuing the development of a career because of the expectation of our culture and society? Was it because of pride? Maybe it was because I have others depending on me? Perhaps it was because I wanted to accumulate wealth? This reflection process caused me to spend a tremendous amount of time evaluating not just what I did, but why I was doing it.

Therefore, I decided to evaluate my life from a reflective perspective in order to discover my purpose in life. I found this evaluation process to be quite different from the normal "mid-life crisis". From what I have observed, men that go through the typical mid-life crisis find themselves escaping into a dream life, rather than figuring out why they are here on this earth.

I hope this book will help you discover your purpose. I believe that once you know why you do what you do, your whole perspective on your life will dramatically change. You will experience a life that is more fulfilling and that your value is not based upon man's idea of worth, but rather on the value God places on your life.

# Chapter One

## What is your life...

Have you ever reflected on your past and pondered your future, only to come up with thoughts of "what really matters"? I recall a time when life was full of exciting things to do with no care for the future. That time was called childhood. During those years, we took one day at a time and looked forward to those all-important events such as a birthday party, Christmas, vacation from school and family outings. It was exciting to get up in the morning during the summer and go fishing, play baseball with our friends, or read a good book (that was not assigned as a school project). We would get so excited when Grandpa would come over to take us to the ballgame or Grandma would invite me to come spend the night at their house. We did things spontaneously.

I remember going out to my grandparents' farm to spend the day playing. We would shoot our BB guns at the birds in the grove, ride on the side of the tractor with Grandpa, or take a hike to the south pasture. It was a great time. I still have a vivid memory of my dad taking me fishing when I was young. The lake was huge and the wind caused the waves to crash into the shore. It was very cold and windy, but I did not care because I was with my father. Dad cast his fishing pole, and all of his line went out of the spool because he forgot to tie off the line. We laughed and laughed. Even though we were very cold and did not catch anything, we had fun.

During those years was I pressured about a house payment coming up or saving for the children's college education? Was I concerned about whether or not my 401K was going to be funded in time for a comfortable retirement? Of course not. My biggest concern was what was for supper.

How things change as we grow older. We find that the "carefree lifestyle" of our childhood quickly vanishes over time. We become teenagers struggling to find our identity in this world while at the same time living up to the new demands and expectations that life puts in front of us. We are now challenged to get good grades and do the best we can in our extracurricular activities such as football, basketball, the debate team or in music. We are thrust into a world of value and worth that is measured by how well we do.

As teenagers we are now faced with responsibilities, which we are held accountable for. For many of us it might have been a car that we had to pay for and all those associated expenses such as maintenance, gas, and insurance. We suddenly discover that the clothes that our parents buy us for school no longer meet with the approval of our peers. Therefore, we go out and purchase new clothes that we think will increase our worth and value in the eyes of others. We feel the pressure to become involved in activities that are not necessarily good for us. The opinions of authority soon disappear behind the cloak of peer acceptance.

In the early seventies I remember when wide belts, bell-bottom pants and platform shoes were the "in thing". Going to school without those was like becoming an outcast. It wasn't long before I obtained a wide belt, bell-bottom pants and platform shoes so that

I could feel as if I was part of the "in" crowd. Peer pressure was so great an influence that it was the primary motivation for everything I did. I went out for high school wrestling and my motivation to excel was so that I would gain the acceptance and worth in the eyes of my peers. I also fell into a life of drugs and alcohol in order to feel accepted. What a devil's trap!

Once we have survived our teenage years we quickly learn that life is full of responsibility and challenges. We are thrust into a world that measures success by upward mobility and ascension into greatness. We live in a society that is advancing faster than we can keep up with. We are now a businessman, attorney, auto mechanic, pilot, engineer, artist or any other label the world puts on us based upon our profession. The pressure to produce "faster, better, cheaper" eventually engulfs our lives.

We now have an employer that continually expects higher levels of productivity and we then expect greater rewards for that productivity. With the greater rewards come greater "I wants" justified by how much we need those wants. We buy a larger home due to the need to have a larger tax write-off. Now that we have a larger home, we need to purchase new furniture to fill the home. What about redecorating the new house because the current wall paper, draperies and paint do not match our tastes. Wow, we now have a three-car garage, therefore, we can buy that new boat or antique car we always wanted! Also, now that we are perceived as being successful in this nicer neighborhood, we need to get rid of that old Ford and get a new Acura.

Our sense of worth and value are solely based upon what others think of us. Remember the story of the prodigal son in the Bible?

He left the security of living with his father, took the inheritance promised to him and squandered it on a lifestyle motivated by the purpose of trying to find himself and gaining the acceptance of others. Are we not the same? We leave the security of our Father in heaven, take the inheritance we are promised and squander it on self-indulgence hoping to gain the acceptance of others.

Have you ever found it interesting that many of our purchases in life are made on emotional appeal and then we find ourselves justifying the purchase after it has been made? We then also find ourselves strapped with the burden of "how am I going to pay for this?" Essentially, we find ourselves in a continuous viscous cycle of never being satisfied and always wanting "more" or "better". Our debt load increases while our peace and joy diminish proportionately. No wonder we live lives that are full of compromise that results in the loss of family, health and peace.

We get up each morning to head off to the office or factory and put in a good day's work. Why, because we need to make money to pay for all the stuff we continually accumulate. After work we come home to enjoy all this stuff only to find that we are too tired and stressed out to enjoy it or we have to fix the stuff that keeps breaking down. After a night of repairing stuff or taking it easy on the lazyboy in front of the television we go to bed and then start all over the next morning. This goes on day after day, year after year after year until our past turns into a blur with little eternal significance.

Now I am not suggesting that the accumulation of "stuff" in and of itself will rob you of your joy and peace. What I am suggesting is that the accumulation (especially <u>over</u> accumulation) can increase the burden and stress caused by the stuff eventually owning you. Perhaps we should evaluate the accumulation of stuff based upon what God desires for our lives rather than what we want.

What about our plans and aspirations for the future? We go to school and gain an education so that we can become the person we envision will make us feel significant and worthy of someone's honor and esteem. We aspire to be that "productive member of society" that our culture encourages. After we have felt some level of accomplishment, we begin to make plans even further into the future such as our children's education and retirement. Time starts to race by and we begin to wonder what worth our lives have accomplished.

Now, am I condemning planning? Of course not. Just think of the tremendous planning it must have taken Noah to build the ark. Or how about all the planning Nehemiah made when he prepared to build the wall around Jerusalem. What about the intricate and detailed planning it took to build the temple? What I am suggesting is that all the planning we do is for whom? I dare say, it usually boils down to satisfying ourselves. We spend our lives planning and pursuing the accomplishment of our plans and along the way we ask God to bless our plans. In James, he says that we "ask amiss" that we may consume it upon our own lusts and selfish desires.

Maslow, a well-known psychologist, suggests that our life over time is like a triangle. At the bottom of the triangle is desire to have our basic needs met (food, shelter, clothing), then the next level is self esteem, then self actualization. At the first level, we spend our lives trying to gain a foothold in this world just trying to meet our most basic needs. Once we have established that foundation of having our basic needs met, we then move onto the level of self-esteem to gain some sense of identity and answer the question "Who am I?" At that level of life we become comfortable with the fact of who we are, which by the way is strongly influenced by what others think. The final and top level of life is self actualization, where we feel a sense of fulfillment in life. The problem with all of this is that "self" is at the middle of this psychology. Where does God come in? What about His plans for our future? How much time do we spend in His Word and in prayer to search and discover what He has in mind for our lives?

God's word really sums up our lives here on earth in James chapter 4. In James 4 verse 14 we are exhorted to examine our lives from an eternal perspective.

- "Whereas ye know not what shall be on the morrow. For what is your life? It is even a vapour, that appeareth for a little time, and then vanisheth away" James 4:14

"...For what is your life? It is even a vapour, that appeareth for a little time, and then vanisheth away". What I see in this verse is that our confidence in the future should not be in what we see or hear. It should not be in "our" future plans. We have no guarantee of even tomorrow. This verse ought to give us the indication of the futility of fretting over the future because we cannot control the future. We often find ourselves putting so much confidence in our employment, intellect, abilities or health when those things have no control or projection of our future. Why not put our confidence in the One who does know and control our future? Our confidence should be in the Will of God for our lives. We need to be

16

constantly and continually seeking God's will. Once we find His will, we need to rest in His will, and then "...occupy until He comes" (or as my pastor, Bob Baier, would say, "do business for the Lord until he returns").

- "And he called his ten servants, and delivered them ten pounds, and said unto them, occupy till I come" Luke 19:13

I heard someone say that an unexamined life is not worth living. Unfortunately we often find ourselves examining life from a perspective of "what's in it for me" whether consciously or unconsciously. Our perspective of upward mobility through the indoctrination of our culture constantly puts us in a position of not being content. Winston Churchill put it well when he said, "We make a living by what we get, but we make a life by what we give". These are some good words to ponder for a while.

Maybe we should be looking at life from a perspective of what we can do for others rather than "what's in it for me". A lawyer friend of mine told me of a divorce case where the man earned almost a million dollars a month. This man was stressed out to the max. He lost his family thinking that if only he could make more money, he would find happiness. Can you imagine the tremendous responsibility just from the shear magnitude of that kind of personal fiscal responsibility and all the people it affected? It appears obvious that he did not find the "peace of God which passeth all understanding" through the accumulation of money.

- "And the peace of God, which passeth all understanding, shall keep your hearts and minds through Christ Jesus" Philippians 4:7

Perhaps, however, if he were motivated to use the talents of generating money as a businessman to support world missions or start an orphanage, he may have found that peace we all long for in our lives. We all either know of someone or have heard of someone that has worked to make their fortune and fame only to find discontentment and unfulfillment.

What I am suggesting is that we take a deeper look into the meaning of life. There has got to be more to life than being born, going through school, getting a good job, making money, buying a house and having a family, funding children's college education, retiring and then dying. Below I try to illustrate this continuum of time, which seems to have no other definition than a continuous cycle that repeats itself. Generation after generation appears to blur over the past with no real significant change to propel us into the future.

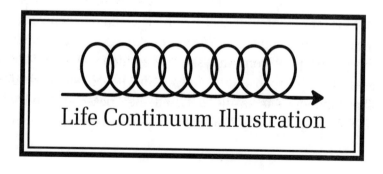

Life Continuum Illustration

I have recently learned from experience that the purpose for your life will not be found in this world, but rather in gaining understanding of what God wants me to do with the gifts and talents he has given me. I do not believe that God intended us to take the pressure for results of this life on our shoulders. Just the contrary is true. In order to live our lives from God's perspective we need to exercise faith. I say exercise because it is a discipline that is developed over time.

Just as Christ stated in the Bible that we need childlike faith to enter the kingdom of God, I believe that it also requires childlike faith to trust your future totally to God and His sovereign will for your life.

- "Verily I say unto you, Whosoever shall not receive the kingdom of God as a little child, he shall not enter therein" Mark 10:15

Go back and recall your childhood and how carefree your life was then. Why was it carefree? Because you were depending upon someone else for your future. We need to depend on our creator for our future, and then, I believe we can experience the peace and joy that God intended for us to experience.

All this, however, assumes that you already have a personal relationship with the Lord. I am not talking about religion. Religion is what **we do**; man trying to get to God. A relationship with Jesus Christ is based upon what **He did** for us.

- "All we like sheep have gone astray; we have turned every one to his own way; and the LORD hath laid on him the iniquity of us all" Isaiah 53:6

Have you come to grips with the fact that you are a sinner, just like every other person?

- "For all have sinned, and come short of the glory of God" Romans 3:23

Do you understand that the punishment for our sin is eternal death, which is separation from God?

- "For the wages of sin is death; but the gift of God is eternal life through Jesus Christ our Lord" Romans 6:23

Therefore, the only way we can gain entrance into heaven and have that relationship with Jesus Christ is to ask him into our heart.

- "Jesus saith unto him, I am the way, the truth, and the life: no man cometh unto the Father, but by me" John 14:6

The Bible explains that if a man believes in his heart and confesses with his mouth, he will be saved.

- "That if thou shalt confess with thy mouth the Lord Jesus, and shalt believe in thine heart that God hath raised him from the dead, thou shalt be saved. For with the heart man believeth unto righteousness; and with

the mouth confession is made unto salvation."
Romans 10:9-10

Saved from what? Saved from an eternity of punishment for our sins in hell. Jesus paid that penalty on the cross for you and me.

God is not looking for great men He can use to advance His cause. I do not find anywhere in the Bible that God sought out men because of their great and noble stature as measured or esteemed by the world's standards. What I remember is God using fishermen (James and Peter), a farmer (Job), a physician (Luke), and a sheep herder (David), etc. Did He pick them because of their great stature in the world? No. He chose them because He was looking for men that would be faithful. Therefore, I believe that God is looking for men who will be committed to be faithful to Him. All He wants from us is to do the best with abilities, talents, resources and opportunities He gives us and then trust Him for the results. He is not holding us accountable for the results. What a pressure relief!

So what is the purpose of your life? Is it to fulfill your ambitions and plans or are you pursuing God's plan for your life? Do you even know what God's plan is for your life? Are you willing to spend the time it will take to search and discover His plan for your life? If so, will you then be willing to commit your life to the purpose of pursuing his plan?

## Chapter 1, questions to ponder:

1.  What takes priority in your life?

2.  What do you spend most of your time doing?

3.  What are your goals and objectives in life?

4.  Why do you think God has placed you here?

5.  What is important to you and how does that match up with what is important to God?

# Chapter Two

# A Different Perspective

A few years ago I had the privilege of going on a missions trip with several men to help a missionary our church supports. I remember the call for help at an October missions conference a year earlier. Our church prepared a men's breakfast where we could spend some time to get better acquainted with our guest missionaries. During that breakfast, Bruce McKee, a missionary to the Philippines, made the plea for several men who would be willing to come to Adams, Philippines to help him finish the construction of a church building. Bruce mentioned that he needed to complete the work he began in Adams so that he could follow God's leading to start a missions work in Cambodia.

Little did I and the other men that went on this trip know, but at that men's breakfast, God spoke to each of us in a very distinct way. Each of us knew that morning that God wanted us to go. I surrendered that morning to go. I had no idea how it would all come together or how God would make it happen. Several weeks after that breakfast each of the men that heard that call to go began sharing how God prompted them. We learned that each of us made the commitment to go that morning. There were 7 of us. God worked out his plan for us all to raise the support we needed. Pastor Jim made all the logistical arrangements and was our "point man" for the trip. We set out to arrive in Manila a year later. Little did we know how God would execute His plan and not our plans that we labored over as we prepared for the trip.

The week arrived that we were set to depart. As I remember it, we were scheduled to leave the Kansas City airport on Friday at 5:50 PM. However, God had a different departure time in mind. I received a call from Pastor Jim at 2:00 PM the day before our departure stating that our departure has been moved up to 6:00 am on Friday. Our flight took us to Chicago, then San Francisco where we had a 9 hour layover. Finally at 11:50 PM we departed to Taipei, China, a 14 hour plane ride. In Taipei, we connected with a flight to Manila, Philippines where we met up with Missionary Bruce. I still remember Bruce's first words. He stated that he could not believe that we really were coming until we actually arrived. Later he told us that many have made commitments to come to the mission field to help him in the past, never to fulfill their commitment.

Our plans continued to be changed by God's divine hand. The next morning we were to take a small (and very old, I might add) turbo prop plane trip to Laoag City, Philippines. However, the pilot did not show up for the scheduled departure. In fact he was 3 hours late. We were quickly learning that our timetable and that of the Filipinos are not on the same clock. By then we were getting a little restless and perhaps a little frustrated because our plans were being delayed.

Once we arrived in Laoag City we were greeted by members of the Northside Baptist Church. It was late at night and we loaded up the jeep with all of our supplies. We joined up with Missionary Bruce, Margaret his wife, and 4 other ladies that were going along to Adams to prepare our meals. Needless to say we were very cramped and over loaded. Not long into the trip, out in the middle of nowhere, we had a flat tire. It turned out that we were so over weight that the rear side panel of the jeep was rubbing into the tire and caused it to blow. "Wow, what do we do now!" Here we were on our way to help God build a church in Adams, (which by the way I think is where God was referring to when he said go to the uttermost parts of the earth) and we got a flat tire, which further delays our plans.

We unloaded the jeep to get to the spare tire and found that we do not have a jack. Well, we finally got the tire changed by manually lifting the jeep while someone changed the tire. We loaded the jeep back up and decided that we needed to lighten the load. Therefore, several of us stayed back to wait for the return of the jeep after supplies were unloaded and the women dropped off at the camp several hours up the road.

Those of us who stayed back decided to start walking down the road. It was pitch black out and we could hear the sound of the South China Sea crashing into the shore. After walking for about an hour we came upon a light in the road where several young people were playing. We walked up to these 17 young people and immediately Missionary Bruce seized the opportunity God had laid in our path and shared the gospel with them. All 17 accepted Christ that pitch black night. We then understood why God caused the delays and trials in our path the last couple days. How awesome are God's plans, even if they first appear to be inconveniences or roadblocks to our plans.

The seven of us packed many tools so we would be prepared to build this church building. We heard that Adams was in a very remote part of the mountainous jungle and that the tools they had were very primitive. When we finally arrived in Adams after hiking for many hours up the mountain and through the jungle we learned what God's plan was for our contribution to the construction of the new church building. We were to move dirt into the building in order to raise the height of the floor by 2 feet. There we were, after traveling for days and over to the other side of the earth, to move dirt. Not only did we move dirt but we also did it by hand! We even tamped the floor by using a wood stump with two sticks nailed to the stump.

God used that dirt moving experience several ways in our lives. First it was humbling, thinking that we had these grand plans of constructing a new church building. Second we discovered again that our plans are not always going to be His plans. And third, it provided a tremendous witness to the people of Adams. They experienced the lives of 7 men that traveled for days at their own expense to "move dirt".

I find that during the course of our lives we spend so much time creating and executing our plans without paying any attention to what God's plans are. When our plans get interrupted or derailed, we immediately get frustrated and angry. In the Bible, James states God has a divine plan for problems that happen in our lives.

- "My brethren, count it all joy when ye fall into divers temptations: knowing this, that the trying of your faith worketh patience. But let this patience have her perfect work, that ye may be perfect and entire, wanting nothing" James 1:2-4

Here James tells us that we should count it "all joy" when we come upon trials or interruptions in our life. Why? Because, God has a greater plan that is much more beneficial to our lives than we could ever imagine. His will and plans are perfect and designed for our benefit. He has an eternal scope or view of things.

Not only did God show me that his plans are much more beneficial than mine, but also that there is a huge world out there that is vast and different than the culture and environment that I grew up in. I experienced lifestyles that are based upon survival rather than materialism. Many of the townspeople of Adams, Philippines live in homes that have dirt floors and open windows with no glass allowing many varieties of critters to enter at their leisure. They have no running water or plumbing. In fact they did not even have toilets, but rather a "squat hole" out back. The villagers laundered our clothes down at the river. The seven of us would bathe by standing in a small basin and pour cold river water over us, lather with soap and then rinse with the same cold river water. Quite a difference from the nice clean hot showers back home. The simple conveniences of life that we took for granted back home were luxuries to the people of Adams.

My accountability partner knows the struggle I experienced the two to three years following that missions trip. After that trip, God began challenging me with various questions. I was miserable with my job, even though I was making more money than I ever dreamed of. When I started "my career" back in 1980, my first year's income was barely over $12,000. The last couple years of "my career" I was making more money than I ever dreamed of making. By the world's standards I was successful. But if that were the case, why was I so miserable? I felt like my life had no meaning, no purpose. The only thing keeping me at my job was the money. The more money I made the more I found it ever increasingly difficult to give up. I was struggling with the so-called balance between materialism and contentment. What I grew to accept as needs in my life, were luxuries by many standards. My views about wants and needs were getting all confused.

The questions God kept challenging me with continued to haunt me. Dr. James Dobson of Focus on the Family articulated these questions very well. I heard him talk about the meaning of life on one of his radio programs. He said his "mid-life crisis" was really a period of "reflective thinking". Questions like "Why am I really here?" or "What does God really want from me?" were confronting him. I was being challenged by the same type of questions; "Why do I do what I do?" and "What is my PURPOSE?" The words to the song, "A Man of God", by Jeoffrey Benword, "it is not what I did, but why I did it and for who" were resounding in my head.

Therefore, the search for God's plan to discover purpose in my life began. I searched for God's plan by spending time reading and meditating on God's Word and spending time asking Him for guidance and wisdom through prayer. I have spent time in God's Word daily for many years, journaling what I thought God was trying to share with me. However, it was not until I started to camp out in a small section of scripture and meditate on that scripture, sometimes even for a few months, that I really began to gain better insight into his plan and purpose for my life.

As I continued to search for God's plan, I remained miserable while I continued on the course of pursuing my career. My job was no longer fulfilling. I kept up a sales pace of over 200% of my sales quota, but I never felt satisfied. My employer was consistently increasing my sales quota every quarter because they were never satisfied either. I began asking myself "When is enough, enough?" Then God finally rescued me. I remember the events very clearly. I went into work one day and found my manager in my office with another associate waiting for me. Immediately I thought, this cannot be good. My boss was never in the office at 7:00 am. She told me that I was terminated effective immediately, with no explanation. Initially I was in shock. Eventually I realized that the reason why I was terminated was that God rescued me from a life of fighting fleshly desires and the besetting sins that was accompanying my lifestyle of pursuing material and financial gain. I was pursuing what the Bible refers to as the lust of the flesh, the lust of the eyes and to pride of life.

- "Love not the world, neither the things that are in the world. If any man love the world, the love of the Father (God) is not in him. For all that is in the world, the lust of the flesh, and the lust of the eyes, and the pride of life if not of the Father, but of this world. And the world passeth away and the lust thereof; but he that doeth the will of God abideth forever." I John 2:15-17

I got caught in the trap of feeling my worth was measured by what I produced and how others esteemed me. I felt unsuccessful if I did not constantly increase my level of productivity. I began to realize that my earthly pursuit through my career did not have eternal significance and that God had a purpose for my life that could impact people for eternity.

I don't think I am alone. I believe that there are many men who feel trapped and that whatever they do today, they are made to feel like it is not going to be enough for tomorrow. Perhaps it is their employer that is never satisfied and always wanting more productivity. Maybe it is a spouse or other family member that has extremely high expectations and you feel like you never measure up. Many men are intrinsically driven, therefore, have tremendously high expectations of themselves, which they never seem to be able to reach. We all in some way find ourselves pursuing someone else's purpose in our lives rather than finding out what purpose God wants us to pursue.

Over the course of the next year, God's plan for my life became evident. He wanted me to take the money that we had been setting aside and use it to start a company that would use its proceeds for world missions. How all of this was to come together was still a mystery to me (and still is I might add), but my wife and I surrendered to his call and continue to trust him for the outcome. As I look back over the past, it is interesting how God's plan for my life was being worked out, even though I did not realize it. For example, we felt that it was God's will that we get out of debt. Therefore, we strived diligently toward that objective for many years. In fact we were only 2 years away from accomplishing our debt free plan when I lost my job. The financial freedom that we now experience through downsizing our lifestyle is totally a God thing. My family and I are full of joy and peace and much happier than when we were making a lot of money. I am now better able to focus on His work rather than be strapped with the stress of financial burdens.

Once I finally understood that God has a greater plan for my life, I asked for God's affirmation. Our church was preparing for our annual missions conference coming up in October. Our Pastor was challenging us to make personal preparation for the upcoming missions conference. I remember after one of his Sunday morning sermons, I went forward to the altar and told God that I needed confirmation of his plan for my life and reveal to me why? I knew that I needed to hear from God and begged him to keep me pure before him during the missions conference so that I would not miss him speaking to me.

Now, was I looking for an audible voice from God? No. I was waiting on the Lord for the peace and joy that comes along with knowing that I am in the center of His will and gaining the understanding of what my life's purpose is. God did affirm His plan and now I am confident about my purpose. After I received the affirmation I was looking for, I developed a purpose statement for the company which essentially states that we will use the results to help send missionaries to the world with the gospel of Christ as well as be available to go to the mission field myself.

Now that I understand my purpose in life, I have been freed from the trappings of this world and the vicious cycle that entangled me. I made that step of "child-like" faith and trusted my entire future, and that of my family, totally into his hands. What is really wild and hard to explain, I do not ever remember a time in my life where I have felt so at peace or experienced so much joy even though I have no idea where my next paycheck is going to come from.

This step of faith required my family to make some tremendous changes, given the lifestyle we were accustomed to. God has used this last 2 years to change my family's perspective of what is really important and what really matters in the eternal realm. He has redefined needs and wants. He has shown us that happiness and joy does not come from the possessions and material gain we used to think would make us happier.

God's plan is what is best for our lives. Therefore we need to search the scriptures, evaluate events and experiences God places in our life from the perspective of His will, seek Him in prayer and look to the guidance of godly council. The American Heritage Dictionary defines **plan** as a "detailed scheme, program or method worked out beforehand for the accomplishment of an objective". It then defines **purpose** as a "result or effect that is intended or desired; intention". I believe that God's plan is what He designed us to do. Our purpose is why we do what we do. Once we discover and understand His plan we then can answer that question of why or "What is my Purpose?"

Consider some of the heroes of the faith in the Bible that knew and understood their purpose in life. The first person in the Bible that comes to my mind is Moses. Moses, by the world's standards had it all. He was adopted into King Pharaoh's family therefore part of royalty. When Moses found out that Pharaoh's army was persecuting his people, he realized that even though he was successful by the world's standards, God had a different plan for his life. God wanted Moses to lead his people out of Pharaoh's captivity and bondage. God revealed clearly His plan to Moses, therefore giving Moses purpose in his life. Take some time to review the life of Moses and look at what God accomplished through the leadership of Moses. How about John the Baptist? Here was a man that from the view of the world was an outcast. He dressed and acted very differently. He may have looked like someone who lived in the streets by today's standards. Yet he knew his purpose in life and he pursued it with ambition and zealousness. God's purpose for John the Baptist was to tell of the arrival of Jesus Christ, who came to pay the ultimate penalty for our sins. Another great example of a person in the Bible was Paul. Paul was a highly educated person and esteemed by others as being very successful. He was driven by his purpose for his life. Before his conversion to Christianity he thought his purpose in life was to persecute Christians. However, when he became a Christian, God gave Paul a new purpose to evangelize the world.

Perhaps God has gifted you with the ability to make money and a lot of it. Great! If that is the case, determine why God has gifted you to make money, then pursue it with all the ability and opportunities God has gifted you with. Maybe God has gifted you as a leader. Why? Maybe it is so that He can use that gift to develop and lead a ministry that will inspire others and exhort others to be more Christ-like. If God has gifted you with the ability to organize and direct musical dramas, then the challenge before you is to discover why.

I recently asked our Minister of Music at church during the Christmas holiday season how he handled the time challenges of all the different programs he was involved in leading (Christmas Dinner Theater, Choir & Orchestra Cantata, children's Christmas play, Candle Light Christmas Eve service, not to mention his normal responsibilities). His answer was refreshing, yet convicting. He said that he looks forward to Christmas because of the opportunity to be involved with all the different events and activities scheduled because that is what Christmas is all about. What an attitude of worship through service! Now, my question was from the perspective of how many of us (including myself) view the Christmas holiday season. We see Christmas as a time of hustle, hurrying, and tremendous time demands, then wonder why we have a hard time experiencing the joy of Christmas. I believe that not only has our minister of music discovered God's plan for his life, but he also understands what his purpose is and why.

Take a look at the life of Christ here on earth. He came to earth with one purpose and that was to die for sinners like you and me. Therefore, He spent His entire 33 years teaching and preparing the way to everlasting life for all who "call upon the name of the Lord".

- "For whosoever shall call upon the name of the Lord shall be saved." Romans 10:13

Consider the fact that Christ had it all. He left the riches, security and peace in heaven to become a man faced with the same trials and temptations as we face. Some of Christ's last words on the cross summarized His life on earth. He said that He came to accomplish the will of His father God rather than His own will. Granted, Christ had the power to call ten thousand angels to rescue Him from the suffering of the cross, but He did not. Why? Because He had purpose!

Another very interesting person with purpose mentioned in the Bible was Mary. Mary understood her purpose when Christ came to visit her and her sister. While her sister, Martha, toiled away in the kitchen thinking that her activity and the accomplishment of her objectives would please Jesus, Mary went and got her most prized and expensive possession, her perfume, and used it to wash Jesus's feet. What an act of worship while serving Christ. Mary's purpose was to worship and glorify Jesus Christ. She strived to exalt Christ and make Him look good. However, on the other hand, like many of us, Martha strived to exalt herself and make herself look good.

The men's ministry leadership team at our church recently evaluated how we can better align the purpose of the men's ministry with the purpose of our church. What we are learning is that God created man to worship him. What we have observed is that we compartmentalize worship as a separate action, usually exercised during a church service, when really, worship should be in all aspects of our life. Worship entails all that we do, think or say. This can be through fellowship, service, evangelism, or discipleship. Worship can also be exhibited at our place of employment and during our recreational activities. Essentially, worship should be central to everything we involve ourselves in.

It is interesting that men will volunteer for a service project due to a feeling of guilt or because someone asked them to. They may feel that if they help with the widows car-care day, they will please God. We often then perform that service as if it were another item on our to do list and then can check off. If we really understood worship, I believe that even our service to others would be done in a way that the world would see that God is great and worthy! If we really understood worship, I believe that we would go to work the next day with a totally different perspective and purpose.

Purpose does not have anything to do with what we do with our lives. It has everything to do with WHY we do it! Perhaps we need to be asking the same kind of questions of ourselves that Dr. James Dobson was asking himself. Maybe we need to evaluate life from an eternal perspective rather than what is best for me. Once we have caught a glimpse of a purpose driven life, I believe we will find the fulfillment we all long for. We will no longer look at life from a perspective of "what I must give up in order to count for something", but rather "how can I invest my life which will pay eternal dividends". A life driven by purpose will enable us to rest at night knowing that what we did that day will have an eternal impact and eternal significance.

The bottom line to all of this is that God's purpose for our lives should revolve around one thing and that is to **Worship and Glorify God** in whatever we do! Worship is acknowledging that God is supreme and above all and the only person worthy of glory and honor. Worship is a lifestyle of subordinating our interests and plans to that of God's. Once we discover why God wants us to do what we do, we will begin to experience the peace and fulfilled life that God intends for us.

The pressure for results is totally lifted off of our shoulders. Our value will no longer be measured by our accomplishments as measured by others. We have purpose for our life and we will experience the fulfillment of the fruit of the spirit as described in God's word.

- "But the fruit of the Spirit is love, joy, peace, longsuffering, gentleness, goodness, faith"
  Galations 5:22

What we do may not even change because you know that what you are doing is what God has designed you to do. However, after you

36

discover why you do what you do, you will do what you do with a whole new perspective because you now have purpose!

Many of us are familiar with the WWJD wristbands. WWJD (What Would Jesus Do?) has become popularized in our society to challenge our motives and behavior in the world today. My Adult Bible Fellowship teacher asked us to consider WWJHMTD (What Would Jesus Have Me To Do?), which I think, is much more personalized, recognizing that God has a specific purpose for us all.

How will those who mean the most to you remember you?

**Chapter 2, questions to ponder:**

1. Who has had the most influence in your life and why?

2. How will you affect your continuum of life?

3. What impact will you make for the cause of Christ?

4. What role have you allowed God to play in your life?

5. What would Jesus have you to do with the rest of your life?

# Chapter Three

## Fellow Strugglers

When we are children our sense of identity and value are based upon our relationship with our parents. Who they are is who we are. It is not until we are thrust into this world that we begin to experience the struggle of seeking who we are as individuals. Usually it is then that we start to look to the world and our society for these answers.

I began to experience this struggle of identity when I was a teenager. There were cliques of teens based upon what they did, what they accomplished or whom they hung out with. I excelled at playing the saxophone in band but that level of achievement was not highly valued by most other teens. It seemed that the highest level of acceptance came from excelling at sports.

Therefore, I tried football. After years of getting the tar knocked out of my 80lb body, I decided that football was not for me! After failing at football, I decided to try wrestling. I stuck with wrestling throughout my high school years and excelled at it. I was getting recognition and a sense of value and worth because of what I did and how well I did. I was quickly learning that in order to increase in value and worth as measured by others, I had to excel at what ever I did.

Another way I tried to find acceptance is by finding that particular clique of teens that I would fit in with. I found that clique when I was in eighth grade. I was offered a joint (marijuana cigarette) and I tried it because I just wanted to fit in. I believed that if I would try it, I would be accepted. Well, I tried it and I was accepted. That decision eventually would almost cost me my life. Throughout high school, I would lay off pot during wrestling, but as soon as wrestling season was over, I went back to those who accepted me, the potheads. I continued to smoke pot and eventually even smoked during wrestling season.

Wrestling, the only other activity through which I found acceptance and value, was the reason I went to college. However, after 2 straight years of knee injuries and major reconstructive surgery on both knees, wrestling was no longer an option for me. That left me with the only other area in life that I found acceptance and value. I started to do more than drink and smoke pot. I became what was commonly referred to back then as a freak. My goal in life was to experience the ultimate party and die by the age of 30. My lifestyle lead to a continual use of LSD and acid.

I remember one night coming back to college after the summer break. I met up with several of my partying friends. I drank a bottle of Jack Daniels and snorted some THP cut with cocaine and crystal speed. As was revealed to me later by a fellow partier the morning after, I stopped breathing that night and they had to revive me by mouth to mouth resuscitation.

Eventually my continued use of drugs put me in the hospital psychiatric ward. It began the summer after my sophomore year in college. I was dropping acid on a regular basis. I began to be paranoid about everything. I left home and went to Iowa City, Iowa. To this day, I still do not know why. After spending a couple of nights sleeping on porches I began to think that the Mafia was after me. I would even read into the horse racing results of the sports section of the local newspaper, code names that identified my family and where the FBI was going to take them for protective custody. I became so paranoid that one night after sleeping in an abandoned car, I rushed to the police office asking for protection. I spent much of that summer in the hospital trying to get my life back. I felt so alone.

Let me ask you a question. Do you ever feel like you are all alone and you are the only one that feels the way you do? Have you ever felt like no one else can relate to the pressures of life that you face day-in and day-out? Do you tend to hold your feelings within? It is a very lonely feeling, isn't it?

Perhaps you have made tremendous strides in your career and you now have personal experience with the phrase "it is lonely at the top". Or maybe you find yourself struggling just to pay your rent and put food on the table for your family. Are you a pastor and feel like you cannot open up and be vulnerable because of the tremendously high moral and ethical expectations that our culture places on you? Maybe you were like me and while seeking to find acceptance, you quickly learned that the acceptance the world offers is fleeting.

Most men I know shoulder the pressures of this world without expressing their feelings about their struggles. Sure we find release in doing other things, but those turn out to be simply a means of escape rather than solutions. We may get involved in a softball league or regularly attend sporting events. Many guys escape to the lake every weekend or a golf course.

However, soon after our retreat into whatever, the next Monday morning we find ourselves faced with the same realities and stress that we tried to find an escape from on Friday. This typical lifestyle of living for the weekend begins to wear on us and we find ourselves just trying to struggle through the week in order to get to the weekend to do what we enjoy doing. Wouldn't it be great if we could not wait until Monday because of the purpose we have in our lives?

How many men do you know that actually go to someone else and open up their lives and become vulnerable by admitting they are struggling? I do not know of many. Why? Because men in our society grow up in a culture that fosters strength and toughness. We are made to believe that if we express any sense of emotion other than rage or anger we are viewed as weak or insignificant. Even when we're small children we are rebuked for crying. No wonder we all look for ways to escape the real world and often find refuge in alcohol, pornography, drugs, affairs, etc. We often find our anger flares at something as insignificant as spilt milk because we have been harboring our feelings inside without any meaningful or expressive release.

Perhaps the reason why there are so many support groups is due to this state of loneliness we experience. There seems to be support groups for everything these days. Not that I am saying there is anything wrong with support groups, however, what does concern me is where many of these support groups go to for solutions.

Now I am not a psychologist, I am just a normal guy like you, but I wonder why we turn to the world and our society by way of these support groups to find answers, when many of the problems we face are a direct result of the negative influence of our current society. Just take for example our airways via television. We have prime time TV filled with shows and advertisements that arouse our flesh. Advertisements promote their products via the passion of "envy". We are influenced to express our feelings of "lust". What happened to the days when television promoted virtue? Now we see it promote promiscuity. We eventually become convinced that the escapes that our society has to offer will fulfill our needs.

In the Bible we are told that there is no problem or pressure point that we experience that is uncommon to man.

- "There hath no temptation taken you but such as is common to man: but God is faithful, who will not suffer you to be tempted above that ye are able; but will with the temptation also make a way to escape, that ye may be able to bear it." I Corinthians 10:13

In fact, many men face the same issues and therefore we are not alone. Secondly, that same verse goes onto say that God has provided a way of escape that will help us overcome these challenges we all face. God may not remove the problem, but He promises that He will enable us to overcome it.

Jesus, in fact, experienced every problem we encounter, yet without succumbing to any one of them.

- "For we have not an high priest which cannot be touched with the feeling of our infirmities; but was in all points tempted like as we are, yet without sin." Hebrews 4:15

Therefore, Jesus understands and can relate to our problems and challenges because He has experienced them as well. This is all the more reason why we should call on Jesus in our time of need.

- "Let us therefore come boldly unto the throne of grace, that we may obtain mercy, and find grace to help in time of need." Hebrews 4:16

Who else better to go to than someone who actually understands and empathizes with our problems than someone that not only experienced the same thing but also overcame it without sin!

You might be asking, "What does this have to do with discovering my purpose in life?" It has everything to do with where you go to discover that purpose. If you go to the world to find your purpose as we often find ourselves escaping in, you will find it feeding the "lust of the flesh, lust of the eyes and the pride of life" (1 John 2:16). You will find yourself pursuing a purpose that has a very short term return on your investment. You will eventually fall for the devils lie that this world can add value to your life. You really end up pursing someone else's purpose at your expense.

After going through the motions of life for many years, most, if not all of us, come to the point where we need to know why we are here. This is so common that our society has labeled this as "mid-life crisis". However, this common thread that many of us share becomes unraveled by where we choose to go to discover the "why am I here?" question. We turn to a friend to find out how they have dealt with this issue. Maybe we spoke with our father about it. Many of us turn to a book, perhaps like this one. I believe that is why Solomon wrote in Ecclesiastes 6 that our wandering desires is vanity and will cause struggles within our spirit.

However, if you go to the Bible to find your purpose in life you will experience the "truth" which will make you "free".

- "And ye shall know the truth, and the truth shall make you free." John 8:32

Your discovered purpose will produce the fruit of the spirit of God: love, joy, peace, patience, longsuffering, temperance, etc.

- "But the fruit of the Spirit is love, joy, peace, longsuffering, gentleness, goodness, faith" Galations 5:22

Therefore, we should be reading the Bible and then thinking (meditating on) about what we read. For example, read through Proverbs. It is full of practical principles that can guide us through the so-called "mid-life crisis". We learn from Proverbs how we can gain wisdom and then apply wisdom. After you have spent some time in the Bible, consider the alternatives this world offers and you tell me where you would best find purpose that will add value to your life and have a positive impact on others for eternity.

What about the struggle of balance? We have all, at one time or another, heard or read about needing to have balance in our lives. The usual areas that are considered include, work, family, church and personal time. There are also many different approaches to managing balance in our lives. As we grow older and our responsibilities change, so to does the pendulum of balance change.

Unfortunately, as men we usually find ourselves getting out of balance in the area of our career. Since our world has a way of determining our value to society by what we do, we are driven to increase our value through our work. How many men do you know that put in enormous amount of hours at work thinking that they are achieving results that will get them ahead? We continue trying to ascend to greatness based upon the world's measure of worth.

As we consider what is proper balance in our lives, who defines what proper balance is? Who should define and direct proper balance in our lives? It will not be until we discover why we do what we do that we will be able to pursue what we do from a foundation of worth and value regardless of what we accomplish. You see, it is not until we measure our worth from God's perspective and quit using the world's yardstick that we will be able to find proper balance in our lives and feel great about it.

God accepts us just as we are and will produce in us who He wants us to be if we let Him. Once we understand and accept the fact that we have great value and worth in God's eyes will we be able to experience a fulfilled life because we are pursuing it with purpose.

Another major issue many men struggle with is past failure. We may have been plagued with the sin of alcohol or drug abuse. Many have been sucked into the fantasy world of pornography, which destroyed their marriages. Others have been duped into believing that the rewards of pursuing a career are worth the price of sacrificing time with their families. Perhaps we got caught up in reaping financial gains fraudulently and paid the consequences.

Our society has a way of using past failures to label us also. Unfortunately, we believe the world and many times accept our new label. However, praise God, He can and will forgive us of our past sins. In fact, the Bible states that if we are a child of God, He will forgive our trespasses. He will cleanse us from all sin.

- "If we confess our sins, he is faithful and just to forgive us our sins, and to cleanse us from all unrighteousness." 1 John 1:9

God not only forgives us of our sins but He remembers them no more.

- "For I will be merciful to their unrighteousness, and their sins and their iniquities will I remember no more." Hebrews 8:12

God will separate you from your sins as far as the east is from the west.

- "As far as the east is from the west, so far hath he removed our transgressions from us." Psalms 103:12

Isn't it great when we are given another chance! God can give us that fresh start. Therefore, when evaluating our lives from the perspective of not measuring up, remember, none of us do.

- "As it is written, There is none righteous, no, not one" Romans 3:10

We all are given second chances through a relationship with our Lord and Savior, Jesus Christ. Christ is the person through which we will find absolute acceptance, just as we are.

In December of 1979 during my senior year of college, my wife and I were in the laundromat doing our laundry when I saw a poster advertising that a Vietnam veteran was going to be speaking at a local church. This caught my attention because I was very interested in learning more about what really went on in Vietnam. I had friends in college that were veterans and was amazed at the stories they told of their experiences. I looked at my wife and suggested that we go, even though it was going to be at a church. We went the next Sunday and heard the story of this veteran's experiences in Vietnam and how they led him to a personal relationship with Jesus Christ. I had heard about the death, burial and resurrection of Jesus before, but it really did not connect with me until that morning. After we left, the veteran's statement of his personal relationship with Jesus kept repeating in my mind. I kept hearing him speak of the unconditional love God offered me through his Son, Jesus Christ. Well, both my wife and I went back to this small church that met in a Knights of Columbus hall. We felt welcome with no one judging us for who we were. We felt accepted just as the Vietnam veteran said God accepted us, unconditionally. A couple weeks later during the end of the service, the Pastor asked if anyone wanted to accept God's gift of eternal life through his son Jesus Christ. I went forward and told the Pastor that I wanted to accept this gift from God. That Sunday morning in December of 1979 I accepted the gift that God offered me. Not only was I given the power of the Holy Spirit to overcome a lifestyle of drug and alcohol abuse, I finally felt accepted unconditionally. I was no longer valued by what I did. I was found worthy by what Christ did for me on the Cross of Calvary when he died for my sins. I later learned that the church I now am a member of and where I have since witnessed my two sons' accepting Christ as their personal savior, helped start this small church.

Once we have been accepted with the assurance that we will never be cast aside, we then can search for our purpose.

- "Let your conversation be without covetousness; and be content with such things as ye have: for he hath said, I will never leave thee, nor forsake thee." Hebrews 13:5

We can develop that relationship with Him by spending time with God. Through that time you will discover your purpose and begin to experience the fulfilled life God has designed for you.

We have tried to find the meaning of life and fulfillment as offered by this world. This world has provided us with so many ways to feed our fleshly desires. Look where it has taken so many of us, living for the weekends week after week after week. Sure, we may have found acceptance, but we soon learned that it was temporary. Don't you think it is time to give Jesus Christ a shot?

**Chapter 3, questions to ponder:**

1. In what have you tried to find fulfillment?  Has it been lasting or was it fleeting?

2. Where have you gone to find the meaning of life?

3. What do you think the meaning of life is?

4. Why do you think God has allowed the various trials in your life?

5. How have those trials affected your life?

# Chapter Four

## What's in it for me?

From the first day of our lives we tend to have the idea that the world was created for our pleasure. We quickly learned that if we cry, our mother or father would quickly come to our rescue and fulfill our need. Maybe it was our diaper that needed changing or we were hungry. Perhaps we just wanted to be held.

How are our lives as men really different from our first days on this earth? From what I observe and experience, it is not all that different. Of course the needs and wants we have are different, but don't we still look at life from the perspective of "what is in it for me"? We tend to evaluate almost everything based upon what we will gain in return for whatever cost or investment is required. Our capitalistic society is even based upon this same principle. It is called ROI (return on investment).

Now, I am not in any way suggesting that we should not be good stewards of our resources. Jesus Christ himself taught the principle of good stewardship in Matthew 25:14-30. The issue here is for whose benefit are we to be good stewards. Unfortunately, it usually works out to be that we do things for our benefit. Sure, we may give lip service to the fact that we are helping some other person or cause, but only after we determine how we can benefit from it.

Self advancement seems like the basis of our existence. We are constantly looking at how we can get ahead and advance for our benefit. We live in a "Burger King" society where we can have it our way. Not only are we getting it our way, we are demanding that we get it faster, better and cheaper. We equate greatness with the advancement of our interests. We believe that we become more valuable to others and ourselves by way of advancement. You likely have seen the bumper stickers, "He who dies with the most toys wins".

This type of lifestyle takes us deeper and deeper into a self gratification cycle that never appears to find its end. We are always wanting more or better. We never seem to be satisfied or content. Once we find out what is behind door number one, we want to know what is behind door number two. What a miserable way to live. God tells us that we are to be content with what things we have.

- "Let your conversation be without covetousness; and be content with such things as ye have: for he hath said, I will never leave thee, nor forsake thee." Hebrews 13:5

Once we understand and live God's principle of contentment, we will have much less stress and much more peace in our lives.

I believe that in our society we have a tremendous "I" problem. What I really find wild is that we may do something really nice for someone else, or perhaps donate something of value to a charitable institution only to appease our conscience of the many pleasures we indulge ourselves in. Even though the act of charity helps someone else, we still may have done it to satisfy self.

Take for example giving to the church. Some may give to the church but then also want to make sure they have a proper accounting of these gifts with the motive that they can use the amount they give as a tax deduction. Again, the issue of stewardship is not in question here. The issue of motive is. Sure, we should take advantage of the tax deductions offered us by our government. But should that be even part of our motive to give?

Another example of the "me first" attitude is exhibited on the freeway. Everyone seems to be in a hurry to get to his destination. You do not dare slow them down by going the speed limit when you are in the fast lane or you may have a few choice words thrown your direction. Or what about when we are in a crowded restaurant and we are not served fast enough. Even though the waitress is working at light speed to serve everyone, there always seems to be someone that will make a scene about not being served to his or her expectation.

What makes us so much more important than the other person? Why is it that our desires should be met before someone else's? Who propelled us to the top of the heap? Unfortunately, this attitude advances our selfish interests usually at the expense of someone else. Our society even has its pecking order based upon the social-economic level we fall into.

It is interesting to observe how we evaluate almost everything based upon what is best for "me". Our interests and pleasure is of the utmost importance. This is exemplified even in our jobs. We might be asked to do something that is outside of our job description. When that happens, what do you think is the first thing that usually pops into our mind? You're right. It is usually "how much will I get paid for doing this?" or "that is not in my job description".

The story of Lot in the Bible (Genesis 13) describes the "what is best for me" attitude. Lot was given a choice to live in the land of Jordan or the land of Canaan. Lot surveyed both options and saw that Jordan appeared to be the better of the two options. Therefore, Lot chose Jordan because he wanted what was best for him. Within the land of Jordan was the city of Sodom. This was a place of self gratification to the max. The people of Sodom were so in love with themselves that they did not leave any pleasure unpursued. We later read that the lifestyle experienced by the people of Sodom eventually brought on their destruction.

Why is it that we live in such a society that promotes a "if it feels good, do it" type of lifestyle? The absence of absolutes, where anything goes, is now normal and you are viewed to be abnormal if you buck this trend. If you stand out of the crowd because of a sincerely held conviction about something you feel is wrong, you will be targeted as being intolerant. Yet, by using their same logic, those who view you as being intolerant are also exercising intolerance by not accepting your view.

Who says that we have to continue along the same path of self gratification? Why can't we live a life that is meant for good and service to others? Philippians 2:3 exhort us to subordinate ourselves to the interests of others.

- "Let nothing be done through strife or vainglory; but in lowliness of mind let each esteem other better than themselves." Philippians 2:3

Wow, just think of how we could turn this world upside down if we would all follow that advice?

Once we have discovered our purpose in our lives, we will then have absolute direction and boundaries that act as our guide through every aspect of our life. Our finances, relationships, morals, ethics, recreation, spiritual and career can be filtered by how they fit within our purpose. As we have mentioned earlier, after you have determined your purpose, you may not change a thing that you are currently doing. What you will change, however, is why you do what you do.

Keep in mind that a central part of your purpose needs to be to "Worship and Glorify God". Remember, that is why we were created. Like the purpose statements we find in corporate America, to propel the interests and investments of its owners, we too, as Christians, ought to have a purpose that advances the cause of Christ, our owner. After all, we were bought with a very costly price, Jesus' death on the cross.

- "For ye are bought with a price: therefore glorify God in your body, and in your spirit, which are God's." 1 Corinthians 6:20

Speaking of corporate America, it is unlikely that you will find a company these days that does not have a mission statement, however many do not have a purpose statement. A mission statement is basically what they are going to do. A purpose statement is why they are going to do what they do. What I suggest we do as men is to develop a personal purpose statement and then develop a mission statement.

As you consider the development of a personal purpose statement, I believe that the first thing you need to do is to seek God's direction and leadership as to what your purpose is. This can be accomplished by spending time in God's word. How else can you truly understand who God is and his wisdom other than spending time with him by reading and meditating on his word? The Bible tells us that all scripture is inspired by God (directly from God) and profitable for our lives.

- "All scripture is given by inspiration of God, and is profitable for doctrine, for reproof, for correction, for instruction in righteousness" II Timothy 3:16

If that is the case, then we should invest much of our time searching its principles.

The apostle Paul nails this principle when he was inspired by God to write Romans 12:1-2.

- "I beseech you therefore, brethren, by the mercies of God, that ye present your bodies a living sacrifice, holy, acceptable unto God, which is your reasonable service. And be not conformed to this world: **but be ye transformed by the renewing of your mind**, that ye may prove what is that good, and acceptable, and perfect will of God." Romans 12:1-2

By spending time with God in his word, we have the promise that he can change our perspective on life from the influences of this world.

David of the Old Testament asked God to open his eyes that he might behold the wonderful truths of God's law.

- "Open thou mine eyes, that I may behold wondrous things out of thy law." Psalms 119:18

We need to have such a thirst for God's Word that the more we spend time with God and the more we learn, the more our thirst increases for more. I suggest that you start your search in Psalms 119. There you will find and gain insight to the value of God's Word through the eyes and heart of David. By spending time in God's word you will find that it is infinite in its wisdom and truth. It is amazing to me that I may have read a portion of scripture many times, but each time I learn something new from it.

Read the stories of biblical characters like Abraham, Moses, Job, David, Paul, etc. As you read about their lives, focus not only on what they did, but why they did what they did. Learn about what the heart's desire was and what motivated them. I think you will find that each one was driven by a God given purpose.

Another very practical way of seeking purpose in your life is by asking God through prayer. Ask God to clear away the distractions in your mind so that you can be more sensitive to God's direction. Ask Him to give you wisdom and provide you with a clear understanding of what His purpose is for your life. The Bible says that if we would only ask God, He will give it to us.

- "And all things, whatsoever ye shall ask in prayer, believing, ye shall receive." Matthew 21:22

- "And whatsoever ye shall ask in my name, that will I do, that the Father may be glorified in the Son." John 14:13

- "If any of you lack wisdom, let him ask of God, that giveth to all men liberally, and upbraideth not; and it shall be given him." James 1:5

Ask God to give you an open mind and heart without the bias of your perspective.

Prayer is the vehicle that God gave us to communicate with Him. It is a tremendous resource that we do not take advantage of enough. The thing that I find so amazing is that you do not need an appointment to talk to God. You can go to Him in prayer anytime, anywhere about anything. There are millions and millions of people on the earth, yet when I talk to God, I feel like I have His undivided attention and sense that what I want to talk to Him about is of extreme importance to Him. It is incredible that our Creator makes time for us.

Finally, seek godly counsel to help you discover your purpose. Find other men of God that you know and that can provide insight and advice.

- "Where no counsel is, the people fall: but in the multitude of counselors there is safety." Proverbs 11:14

- "The way of a fool is right in his own eyes: but he that hearkeneth unto counsel is wise." Proverbs 12:15

- "Without counsel purposes are disappointed: but in the multitude of counselors they are established." Proverbs 15:22

- "Ointment and perfume rejoice the heart: so doth the sweetness of a man's friend by hearty counsel." Proverbs 27:9

Surround yourself with men that will inspire you. Something that I learned along time ago is "show me your friends and I will show you your future". I do not remember when I first heard this, but I have heard it many times over the years and it has stuck with me. I enjoy being around people that challenge me. I have a friend that is a relatively new Christian, yet his servant's heart and hunger for God's word makes my desire for the same seem like I am nibbling. I enjoy serving with him because every time I am with him I get convicted about being a better servant and student of God's word.

I also enjoy being around missionaries. Missionaries are heroes of the faith. I recently heard a definition of hero that I really liked; a hero is someone that is driven by a noble purpose. I receive a tremendous challenge from God by being around them. They are not only seeking God with all their heart, mind and soul, they also trust their entire lives and future to God on a day-by-day basis. I know of very few men that are that committed to their relationship to God. During our most recent mission conference, the guest speaker challenged us to do something for God that only can be accomplished by God. Our Pastor made the same challenge and that was to be a water-walker for God, referencing Peter's experience in Matthew 14.

The people you surround yourself with can help you see the forest while the tree in front of you blinds you. They can help you identify your gifts and talents that God has blessed you with. Godly counsel can also warn you about going down the wrong path or making a decision that could be very detrimental to you and your family.

Once you have discovered your purpose in life write it down and carry it with you in your billfold. After you have determined your purpose, develop your mission statement. Determine what you are going to do and how you are going to do it. Your mission statement will give you direction. It will help you establish goals and objectives that are in line with your purpose. Make sure, however, that your mission is guided by your purpose. Your **mission** is **what** you plan on doing. Your **purpose** is **why** you do it.

This process will take some time, as it should. Once you have identified your purpose, write it down on a piece of paper. You may want to have it laminated and put it in your billfold. Refer to it often, especially those times that you feel disoriented or discouraged. Make your purpose statement a part of your everyday prayer life, asking God for wisdom and direction in fulfilling your purpose. Use it to filter everything you encounter. Make every decision based upon how it will reflect on your purpose.

You maybe asking, well this sounds good, but wondering what my purpose is. I am glad you asked. My purpose is to Glorify God in all that I do as he enables me to be used in continuing the work of Jesus Christ through world missions. This is also the purpose of the business that God has allowed me to develop. I am looking forward to how God is going to use this business to help further the cause of Christ through world missions. It is very exciting and fulfilling to be a part of God's plan that pays eternal dividends. The rewards for having a purpose that has an eternal impact on people will never diminish. After God has given me this purpose, everything that this world has to offer has paled by comparison. All the stuff in the world has become less and less important as I have pursued the purpose God has given me. In addition, the pressure for producing results has been decreasing while the peace of God in my life has been increasing.

**Chapter 4, questions to ponder:**

1.  Why do you go to work?

2.  Why do you go to church?

3.  What have you wanted to gain out of life and is it in line with what God would want?

4.  What investments have you made for the future and what affect will these investments have on eternity?

5.  What is your God given purpose?

# Chapter Five

## If you want to be great!

I do not know many men that do not aspire to be great at something. Whether it be to accomplish a feat that no one else has been able to achieve or be the best in some area, we seem to gain tremendous esteem and sense of worth by what we are able to accomplish as I mentioned previously. Regardless of why we want to be great, we all seem to want to count for something.

Think about those that you recognize as being great. Names like Teddy Roosevelt or Abraham Lincoln may come to mind. Or how about sport figures like Hank Aaron or more recently, Michael Jordan and Tiger Woods. Maybe your thoughts reflect on the achievements of people like Bill Gates or other successful business people.

The common thread of all of these men like many others is that they are remembered by their achievements. I am sure that there are many great character qualities that these men have. However, what we remember about them is their level of accomplishment. For example, Michael Jordan is known as a great basketball player and Bill Gates as a great businessman in the technology industry. What they accomplished reflects their level of greatness.

We live in a world that puts high value on what we do. However, God puts great value on who we are. There is a huge difference in the two. Our society elevates those who achieve, whereas, God elevates those who are humble and meek and who subordinate their own interests for the benefit of others.

- "Let nothing be done through strife or vainglory; but in lowliness of mind let each esteem other better than themselves. Look not every man on his own things, but every man also on the things of others." Philippians 2:3-4

- "And whosoever shall exalt himself shall be abased; and he that shall humble himself shall be exalted." Matthew 23:12

Take a look at the life of Job. Sure, he was wealthy and an achiever from the world's perspective. He possessed great numbers of livestock and a tremendous amount of land. He also had a large family. By the world's standards, he was very successful. However, God used the life of Job to illustrate his faithfulness and commitment to God even after losing everything that the world put high value on. Satan wanted to attack Job hoping to prove to God that the only reason Job was "perfect and upright, and one that feared God and eschewed evil" was because of the great wealth that God allowed Job to experience.

God allowed Satan to attack Job resulting in Job losing his wealth, family and health. Job even lost the esteem of his friends and wife. However, not once did Job turn his back on God. He still worshipped God, and even in the midst of his tremendous trial, Job fell to the ground and worshipped God. What a contrast to many of us. When we are faced with adversity, we usually cry out to

God, "why me?" or "help me!" rather than worshipping, praising and glorifying God.

I recently read a devotion that really challenged me in the area of offering praise and thanksgiving to God. I (and I am sure many others) often go to God in the midst of trials and problems asking for relief and deliverance. However, I need to remember that God has a purpose for the trial and problem, which we have no concept of. Therefore, I need to offer praise and thanksgiving to God for the trials, recognizing that he will use the trials to help me be a better Christian.

Many times we are blinded by the trees in front of us, rather than considering the view that God has of the forest. I look back over my past and can now see why and how God used trials in my life to grow me and stretch my faith. Therefore, during trials and testings, I should praise God and thank him, knowing that he is refining his gold.

- "Wherein ye greatly rejoice, though now for a season, if need be, ye are in heaviness through manifold temptations: that the trial of your faith, being much more precious than of gold that perisheth, though it be tried with fire, might be found unto praise and honour and glory at the appearing of Jesus Christ" I Peter 1:6-7

Another example of a great man in the Bible is Paul. Paul was a man of tremendous social and economic stature. He was an educated man and felt that his purpose in life was to persecute Christians. He diligently sought after the destruction of the

Christian faith. But, read on. Look at what God did in his life once God got Paul's attention on the road to Damascus. Paul used the same zealous qualities, which God blessed him with, for the cause of Jesus Christ. Paul turned his world upside down for his new purpose and that was to worship and glorify God by persuading people about their need for Christ in their lives.

Jesus Christ is the best example of greatness. His greatness is not based upon the many miracles he performed, or the tremendous following he has. I believe his greatness is based upon his willingness to subordinate his own interests and comforts for the interests of others.

Jesus Christ did have it all. In fact Jesus Christ, being God himself, left a perfect and wonderful home in heaven to come DOWN to this earth for one purpose. That purpose was to die so that we could live. Jesus Christ was not interested in self advancement. In fact, Jesus Christ leaves behind the legacy of the truest sense of descending into greatness as described in Bill Hybels book "Descending into Greatness".

Jesus paid the ultimate sin penalty for you and me with the humility of dying on the cross. Christ suffered a martyr's death. Take a few moments and reflect on the significance of that event in history that dramatically changed the destiny and eternal hope for mankind. No other person subordinated his or her own interests for the benefit of all.

Jesus gives us a great picture of being great through the act of service. When Jesus gathered the disciples in the upper chamber for the last Passover (read John 13: 1-20), He did what was customary at the time when you had guests at your home. You would offer a basin of water and a towel for your guest to wash his feet. However, Jesus went even further and took the basin of water and a towel and began to wash the disciples' feet. What a tremendous example of humble service. Why did he do this? He wanted the disciples to know that if they wanted to be great, they needed to surrender their own interest and comforts to serve others.

What Jesus, Paul and Job have in common was the surrender of their rights. They are examples of their total commitment to God by turning over to God everything in their lives. They, like many others in the Bible, gave up everything so they could be servants of God. In fact, their lives were living examples of God's definition of greatness.

Otto Koning teaches a great method of surrendering our rights. In his method of "Yielding our Rights" (see illustration on page 68) he creates a circle that is split into a pie shape with the altar of God at the center. Each piece of the pie represents an area of our lives: Body, Time, Health, Possessions, Talents, Family and Friends, Reputation, Future.

I have something in common with Otto. I like order and process which helps me execute plans and ideas. What I did with Otto's method of yielding our rights was to write down the date that I surrendered that piece of my life to God. This gave me an orderly process and a means of reference so that both God and I knew I was serious.

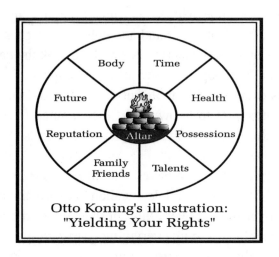

Otto Koning's illustration:
"Yielding Your Rights"

In Otto Koning's brochure "Yielding our Rights", he gives biblical examples of others who gave up their rights, which God used to advance His kingdom. Abraham gave up his right to choose what country and fields he would like to have had.

- "And Abram said unto Lot, Let there be no strife, I pray thee, between me and thee, and between my herdmen and thy herdmen; for we be brethren. Is not the whole land before thee? Separate thyself, I pray thee, from me: if thou wilt take the left hand, then I will go to the right; or if thou depart to the right hand, then I will go to the left." Genesis 13:8-9

The result was Abraham becoming the father of God's great nation and he became very wealthy. Ruth gave up the right to be married (Ruth chapter1-4), which resulted in her being married to the best of all, Boaz. Job gave up the right to material possessions and to own things (Job chapter 1), which resulted in God giving him twice as much as he originally had. Finally Jesus gave up his right to his reputation (Philippians 2:5-11), which resulted in the hope of heaven for all mankind through the finished work of Jesus Christ.

What I soon learned is that after surrendering each area of my life, God tested my commitment. As an example, I remember in December 1992, I surrendered my career to God. On January 2, 1993, less than a month later, I was terminated from my job because of the position was being eliminated. Wow! God wanted to know if I really trusted him for my future and career. As it turned out, 3 months later I was offered a much better position back in Kansas City, which enabled me to eventually discover and pursue God's purpose in my life.

In John 12:24-25, Jesus said that "...Except a corn of wheat fall into the ground and die, it abideth alone: but if it die, it bringeth forth much fruit. He that loveth his life shall lose it; and he that hateth his life in this world shall keep it unto life eternal." In other words, we must die to self and selfish interests in order to understand and experience the prosperity principle. Jim Elliot once said, "He is no fool who gives what he cannot keep to gain what he cannot lose".

What are some truths that we can learn from surrendering our rights? One, I believe, is that God will meet our needs. God promises to take care of His own. In Matthew 6:31-34 we are instructed that if we put God and His righteousness first in our lives our needs will be met. Our interests and rights need to be subordinated to God's interests and rights in our lives. Jesus Christ referenced the lilies of the field and how they do not work for their survival but God takes care of their needs (sunshine, fertile soil, water and air). He goes on to say that we are much more precious to God than the lilies and if God can take care of those plants, how much more He is able and interested in taking care of our needs (Matthew 6:25-34).

God also promises that he will supply all our need according to his riches as written in Philippians 4:19. I noted in my Bible a word-by-word breakdown of this verse that helps me better understand and apply this promise. The word "but" indicates to me the hope of future and absolute joy. "My" gives me the assurance that God's promise is personal and possessive. "God" illustrates power, and the fact that I must exercise belief and faith. The word "shall" communicates a level of performance, which is conclusive and decisive. "Supply" represents provision, "all" equates to plenty and abundance. The word "your" reinforces the personal nature of God's promise and "need" represents our life's necessities. "According to his riches in glory" tells me that I have access to everything that God owns and He owns it all. The phrase "by Christ Jesus" tells us by what process He will deliver this promise.

Another truth that I have learned is that God will test our commitment to surrender. As illustrated by James 1:2-4, God will allow trials that involve various aspects of our life in order to teach us spiritual lessons and help us mature spiritually.

- "My brethren, count it all joy when ye fall into divers temptations; knowing this, that the trying of your faith worketh patience. But let patience have her perfect work, that ye may be perfect and entire, wanting nothing." James 1:2-4

It has been encouraging to me to look back at certain trials God has taken me through in the past to see how He has used them to help me grow up in the Lord and trust Him with even more of my life. The absolute proof that God is still with me and will never forsake me is in the fact that as soon as He has taken me through the fire in one area in my life and taught me a spiritual lesson, He finds another area in my life that needs changing.

The final truth that is more experiential is that our prayer life will be filled with praise and glory to God even during the times of trial, rather than pleading for Him to deliver us from the trials. My family and I recently went through a major downsizing in our lives. Everything from the house we lived in, vacations we took to the place where we buy our groceries has significantly changed. What is really wild is that we are much happier and have much more joy in our lives than we have ever experienced before. I cannot explain this other than by the unspeakable joy and peace that God has filled our hearts with.

Do you want to be great? If so, what do you need to surrender in order to accomplish greatness. What are the "buts" or "ifs" that are keeping you from stepping up and letting God run your life. As long as we go through life trying to advance our own interests for our own benefit, we will never achieve lasting greatness. If we continue to live our lives by our plans and agendas we will continue to be remembered by what we did, not who we are.

**Chapter 5, questions to ponder:**

1. Who in your life have you known that has exemplified servanthood and how?

2. Who serves you and how?

3. Who do you serve and what is your motive?

4. What rights have you yet to give up?

5. Describe what you think biblical servanthood is and why it would probably be a part of any purpose God has for our lives.

# Chapter 6

# Inhibitors

We live in a society and culture that is constantly striving to get our attention. By just driving down the road we are bombarded with billboards crying out "Look at me!", "Check this out!", "Wow, doesn't this look great!". Advertisers are very aware of the fact that everything we do is initiated by some kind of motivator, whether unconsciously or intentionally. Commercials and advertisements effectively use these motivators to capture our attention, gain our interest and then influence our decisions. It is interesting to examine how these motivators are used to persuade and influence people to do something.

Motivators influence and they can become huge inhibitors to following our God given purpose in life. Some of the motivators I am referring to are Security, Fear, Money and Esteem. Each one of these motivators is very powerful. They have been used to build powerful governments, create huge corporations, and accomplish national titles. However, these motivators can become inhibitors when we become overly focused and driven by them. Our world system and culture knows this and uses these for its own benefit.

Take security for example. Everyone wants to feel secure. This basic need begins when we are young. We feel secure when we are with our family and have a home to live in. We build up a comfort zone surrounded by our friends and family and do not like having to move to a new town because it shakes up that security blanket we have within that circle of family and friends. Then we move into adulthood, where many of us find security in our jobs. We want to know that if we work hard, we will be able to continue to provide a good home and lifestyle for our children. Next we start considering the security of our future. Therefore, retirement plans and health care become a priority. We want to feel comfortable that we will have the security of an income to be able to live on once we hang up our work clothes.

Yes, security is important, but in whom or what are we placing our security? In my business I often ask what a person is looking for in their next job. It amazes me that, frequently, their answer is they are looking for security. I go on to ask how they assess or define security. Many of the responses are based upon the financial health and market strength of the company they work for. They are placing their security in "who" they work for. Pretty interesting, especially given the fact that during the most recent recession millions of employees lost their jobs working for so-called "secure" companies. How many men do you know today that start working with a company right out of school and stay there until they retire? The only men that I remember staying at one company during their working lives is within my father's generation.

Remember the Allstate commercials. They would say "You're in good hands", communicating the sense of security you have by giving them your insurance business. How many of us have life insurance, thinking that this type of insurance is going to provide our family with a secure future if we were to die? Sure, that may be good stewardship in taking care of your family in the case of your death, but how sure are you that it will provide your family with so-called security. What about auto, home and health insurance? We pay our premiums every month to a company that can only make money by playing the odds that their insurance payouts will be less than premiums paid. I am not suggesting that we do not have these types of insurances. What I am suggesting is that we consider them for what they are, a hedge against financial loss. They are not, however, guarantees of security.

Security is big business. You have companies that sell and install security systems for your home, business, and cars. What about internet and computer security? Our airports are becoming increasingly security conscious ever since the September 11th terrorist attacks on the United States. Why is it then that our world becomes more and more unsafe and crime continues to increase even though we increase security surrounding us with more and more protection? Are we really becoming more secure because of the advancement and marketing of these so-called security systems?

Our problem is that we are looking to the wrong resource to provide us the security we want. We will never gain the security we long for outside of the relationship we have with God through His son Jesus Christ. Once we realize that our security is in Christ, we will then be able to focus on God's purpose for our life and execute his plan without having to worry about tomorrow. Wouldn't it be great not having to be concerned about our security? "God is our refuge and strength..." Psalms 46:1. Solomon wrote in Proverbs 1:33 "But whoso hearkeneth unto me shall dwell safely, and shall be quiet from fear and evil".

Another inhibitor that will derail us from pursuing God's purpose in our life is fear. This was a big one for me. Many years ago, I was led by God to start a men's ministry. I struggled with this because I did not feel that I had the capabilities to develop such a ministry at the church I attended. Therefore, I ran from this prompting by God. After several years of fleeing, I finally surrendered to God, trusting that if he really wanted me to start a men's ministry, the results had to be up to Him and all I needed to do was to take full advantage of the resources, abilities and opportunities He gave me. That was in 1993. We now have a thriving and growing men's ministry at the church I attend; not as a result of me and my efforts, but because I was willing to yield and trust God, even though the feat seemed very scary.

That experience reminded me of Moses. He felt very ineffectual because he was not a great speaker with tremendous charisma. I identified with him because, I believe that I am not effective or comfortable in front of large audiences, nor do I feel that I am worthwhile to listen to. However, God pulled together a group of men to lead the men's ministry, each with his own God-given abilities, complementing the leadership team.

Because of this experience and other events God has taken me through, it was much less intimidating for me to start a company whose purpose is to generate capital for supporting world missions. I believe that I am privileged to be used by God in such a way and totally trust Him that He will take care of my family's needs and raise money for world missions. This, by any standards, was and still is, a huge risk. Even though I have yielded to God's purpose in my life, trusting him completely, I still struggle with fear. I fight the fear battle of, "is this going to work?", or " am I doing the right thing?". Questions like "What if this really is not God's purpose for me?" really diffuses my focus.

When we started the company, I shared our vision and mission with some friends at church. What surprised me is that I was faced with some critics that said that no one would want to do business with a company that promotes itself as a Christian company with Christian principles and objectives. What was cool though, God, at that very moment reassured me with the thought "if a company does not want to do business with you because of the Christian principles promoted by your company, then perhaps you should not be doing business with them anyway". Boy, did I get pumped up and even more excited!

There is the real sense of fear if we are to pursue God's purpose in our lives that most, if not all of us want to avoid. Perhaps, in your search for God's purpose in your life God wants you to sell your home and all you possess to follow him as a missionary in a foreign country. Remember what Jesus said to the rich young ruler in Matthew 19:21?

- "Jesus said unto him, If thou wilt be perfect, go and sell that thou hast, and give to the poor, and thou shalt have treasure in heaven: and come and follow me." Matthew 19:21

After the rich young ruler acknowledged that he has kept God's commandments with the motive of attaining eternal life, Jesus challenged him with the fact that his dependence on his worldly riches were still holding him back from eternal life. Jesus challenged him to dispose of his riches (dependence on his wealth) by giving all that he had to the poor and then accepting Christ as his savior and making God the Lord of his life. Unfortunately the rich young ruler was so caught up in his wealth that he could not leave it, fearing perhaps the risk of following Christ.

- "But when the young man heard that saying, he went away sorrowful: for he had great possessions." Matthew 19:22

God's purpose in your life may not require such an extreme step of faith right now. Maybe His purpose in your life is as simple as walking across the street to share what God has done in your life to your neighbor.

These are real fears that can cause tremendous anxiety. What I have learned and experienced, though, is that when we step out in faith onto that limb way out on the edge of the tree, God gives us reassurances and affirms us along the way that we are on target and that He will take care of us and complete the work He began in us (Philippians 1:6). Following God is an act on our part that requires faith. We need to exercise faith to overcome the fears of what we call risk in order to pursue God's purpose in our life. We need to trust that we have no fears that God cannot give us victory over. Proverbs 3:5-6 states, "Trust in the Lord with all thine heart; and lean not unto your own understanding. In all thy ways acknowledge him, and he shall direct thy paths". Who better to direct your paths, than the God who created, owns and rules over everything!

As the story of the rich young ruler illustrated above points out, a third area that can be an inhibitor to the pursuit of God's purpose in your life is money. Money can become a central and most important issue if we let it. If we are in debt, being able to make payments to our creditors can produce tremendous anxiety. We are also bombarded by so many investment options each projecting various returns on our money. Many of us are wise enough not to fall for the "get-rich-quick" promises, however, are we exercising wisdom by placing so much faith in other so called "safe" investments?

What if we were to experience another stock market crash, or our government declares a state of financial insolvency? We are lead to believe that there are too many governmental safe guards protecting us from such occurrences, but how can we be so sure? Take for example the investment you have made on your home. Most of us have a mortgage, presuming on the future to be able to eventually pay off that debt. What if you lose your job, or experience unexpected health problems that inhibits or keeps you from working, therefore making it impossible to make your mortgage payments? You risk not only the loss of your home but also all the money you invested into that home.

For example, if you lose your job and can no longer make your mortgage payments, even if you have already paid off $180,000 of a $200,000 mortgage, the mortgage company can repossess your home and you would lose everything you paid into that home.

Remember reading about the stock market crash in the 1930s? Larry Burkett does a great job of illustrating these potential risks in his book "The Coming Economic Earthquake". The Bible also warns us about debt. In the Bible, God does not forbid debt, but He gives very strong warnings about debt. In fact, God uses a pretty strong illustration about debt by stating we are slaves to those who we are in debt to.

- "The rich ruleth over the poor, and the borrower is servant to the lender." Proverbs 22:7

The Bible has much to say about money and the management of it. I believe God knew it could be a tremendous issue for us. What we need to be cautious of, however, is that we do not let money and the management of it overcome our pursuit of God's purpose in our lives. Surely, we need to have proper stewardship over money issues, but not to the extent that we become blinded to the overall purpose God has for our lives. Financial issues can become daunting to say the least. If we follow the instructions given by God in His word, we will be successful in our financial affairs, therefore, removing money from being an inhibitor to following God's purpose in our lives.

The fourth primary area that can overshadow discovering and executing God's purpose in our lives is seeking the esteem of others, sometimes commonly referred to as ego or pride. As we mentioned earlier, we all want to be accepted and approved, however, when we seek that acceptance and approval from people rather than from God, we can quickly become disappointed. It is very easy to get caught up in the trap of acceptance based upon performance. It seems that in our world our acceptance is solely based upon performance. Maybe that is why most people think that the path to eternal life and heaven is based upon our good works. Fortunately, Jesus provides us with the gift of eternal life based upon His finished work on the cross, and it is NOT based on our works (Ephesians 2:8-9).

- "For by grace are ye saved through faith; and that not of yourselves: it is the gift of God: Not of works, lest any man should boast." Ephesians 2:8-9

What we need to realize is that our lives are not about ourselves with the motive of "look at me". Rather, our lives should be in the pursuit of executing God's purpose, which will cause others to see Christ and His likeness in our lives. Peter exhorts us in I Peter 5:6 to subordinate our interests to God's interests and then He will exalt you in His time.

- "Humble yourselves therefore under the mighty hand of God, that he may exalt you in due time" I Peter 5:6

I wrote in the margin in my Bible by this verse, "path to promotion". You see if we seek to enhance the reputation of God and esteem Him, God will see to it that we will be approved and accepted in a way that this world could never deliver to.

If we are to discover and pursue the purpose that God gives us, we need to guard our hearts and minds against these and other inhibitors. They can not only diffuse our focus, but also completely derail our lives, thereby, rendering our lives inoperable and ineffective in carrying out God's perfect will for our lives. If we succumb to these distractions, we will never experience the complete joy and peace that God has to offer us.

**Chapter 6, questions to ponder:**

1. What are you depending on for your sustenance?

2. What would you do or how would you change the way you live if your income was interrupted for a period of time?

3. What fears do you wrestle with that should be given over to God and His power to overcome?

4. How much influence does money play in your life?

5. Whose esteem are you trying to win?

# Chapter 7

## Peace That Passeth All Understanding

If I were to offer you $10,000 with no strings attached, would you take it? What if I said that there was one condition. What if that condition was that if you took the $10,000 you would have to give back to me all the cares and concerns that you have in your life.

More than likely your response would be "WOW! What a deal. Not only do I get a large amount of money, but in addition, I get someone that will shoulder all of my cares and concerns". Sound too good to be true? Well, it is not. In fact, that is exactly the life God promises if we are only willing to discover our purpose in life and then be obedient to His word in executing that purpose. Read Romans 8:28.

- "And we know that all things work together for good to them that love God, to them who are the called according to his purpose." Romans 8:28

In this passage of scripture we are told that all things work together for good to them that **love** God and are called according to his **purpose**. In Philippians 4:6-7 God promises peace that is beyond our comprehension and understanding if we would only talk to God about our needs through prayer.

- "Be careful for nothing; but in every thing by prayer and supplication with thanksgiving let your requests be made known unto God. And the peace of God, which passeth all understanding, shall keep your hearts and minds through Christ Jesus." Philippians 4:6-7

Picture the cross for a minute and what it represents. The cross is the bridge that God used to sacrifice his Son in order to give us access to a heavenly home as well as a direct line of communication by prayer with God through Christ. Jesus not only paid the penalty for our sins, but because of His death, burial and resurrection, we now are "joint heirs" of all that God has to offer us.

- "And if children, then heirs; heirs of God, and joint-heirs with Christ; if so be that we suffer with him, that we may be also glorified together." Romans 8:17

- "Hearken, my beloved brethren, hath not God chosen the poor of this world rich in faith, and heirs of the kingdom which he hath promised to them that love him?" James 2:5

- "That being justified by his grace, we should be made heirs according to the hope of eternal life." Titus 3:7

We now have access to the riches of God while at the same time a relationship with someone that we can share our concerns with, trusting that He will take care of us. What a deal! Tell me, where else can you go to get such a great proposition.

Now, I am not suggesting here a message of health and wealth. What I am suggesting is that if we truly want to experience the undeniable and complete peace of God, we need to discover God's purpose for our lives and then live in obedience to God's word by, as Bill Hybels said, "becoming fully devoted followers of Jesus Christ". In other words, find out what God's purpose is for your life and then execute it as a committed follower of Jesus Christ.

Once we have discovered God's purpose for our life, we now need to execute it. However, we will not experience the complete peace of God if we execute our new God given purpose outside the confines of the local church. Let's look at I Peter 2:4.

- "To whom coming, as unto a living stone, disallowed indeed of men, but chosen of God, and precious" I Peter 2:4

Here, Peter tells us that Jesus Christ is the living and precious stone used by God (even though he was rejected by men) to be the foundation of the church. Peter goes onto say that we as Christians are also living stones and used to build up the "spiritual house" (church).

- "Ye also, as lively stones, are built up a spiritual house, an holy priesthood, to offer up spiritual sacrifices, acceptable to God by Jesus Christ." I Peter 2:5

Therefore, the church is the vehicle through which we are to carry out the overall purpose of every Christian, and that is to worship and glorify God by offering up sacrifices that are acceptable to God. Ephesians 3:21 states that we glorify God in the church through Jesus Christ.

- "Unto him be glory in the church by Christ Jesus throughout all ages, world without end. Amen." Ephesians 3:21

In his commentary, Matthew Henry says that the church is a "sacred society constituted for the glory of God".

Peter is exhorting us to do everything for the glory of God through the local church because we are a living part of the church. In fact God's purpose for a Christian will always be best fulfilled when it is connected with the local church. God ordained the local church so that He would have the platform to accomplish His will for evangelism, baptism, discipleship, worship and fellowship.

- "And I say also unto thee, That thou art Peter, and upon this rock I will build my church; and the gates of hell shall not prevail against it." Matthew 16:18

Therefore, if we feel our purpose is to be executed outside the confines (authority of) the local church, then there is a high likelihood that the purpose is from man and not God.

In addition, to experience the peace that passeth all understanding, we need to trust that God's purpose for our life is what is best for us. Peace = trusting God. Solomon states it best in Proverbs 3:5-6.

- "Trust in the LORD with all thine heart; and lean not unto thine own understanding. In all thy ways acknowledge him, and he shall direct thy paths." Proverbs 3:5-6

Who best to put your complete trust in than the all knowing, all-powerful and all present God.

In Jeremiah 9:23-24 we are encouraged not to follow after or depend upon the wisdom, wealth or strength of man but rather seek understanding and knowledge from God.

- "Thus saith the LORD, Let not the wise man glory in his wisdom, neither let the mighty man glory in his might, let not the rich man glory in his riches: But let him that glorieth glory in this, that he understandeth and knoweth me, that I am the LORD which exercise lovingkindness, judgment, and righteousness, in the earth: for in these things I delight, saith the LORD." Jeremiah 9:23-24

Jeremiah 10:23 states that knowledge of our future is not in man, but in God.

- "O LORD, I know that the way of man is not in himself: it is not in man that walketh to direct his steps." Jeremiah 10:23

Psalms 32:8 says "I (God) will instruct thee and teach thee in the way which thou shalt go: I will guide thee with mine eye". Once you have identified God's purpose for your life, you must execute it while trusting God in order to truly experience peace.

Once you have your purpose defined, put together a plan of action that you will follow to execute your purpose. I have experienced how the pressure to produce results has disappeared, but the drive to work hard taking full advantage of the opportunities, abilities and resources God has provided becomes more and more inspirational. God wants us to do the best we can as managers of the time, money, and abilities He has given us. However, we need to leave the results up to God. One thing you need to remember, even though your purpose may be static and never change, what you do to execute your purpose must be dynamic, flexible and adaptable. What you do may change, but why you do what you do should not change if your purpose is to Glorify God.

As you may already have picked up on by now, God's primary purpose for our lives is to glorify Him in all that we do, think or say. Under that umbrella, God has a specific purpose for each and every individual as unique as we are different. God has gifted each of us with specific talents and capabilities. I Corinthians 12:27 states that we (the church) are the body of Christ, members in particular.

- "Now ye are the body of Christ, and members in particular." I Corinthians 12:27

The scriptures also explain in I Corinthians 12:12-31 that each Christian has a gift and not all having the same gifts and that each gifted Christian is important to the total functioning of the body. No one capability within the church is more important than the other. Each is needed in order to complete the body for God's use.

Therefore, since we understand that God's ultimate purpose in life is to glorify Him, we need to discover what gifts and talents God has given us so that we can discover our individual purpose and role within the church. At the church I am a member of, we all take a spiritual gifts inventory. This is helpful to gain a perspective on what you are good at and enjoy doing. Some find that their gift is hospitality. They enjoy and are gifted at greeting people and making them feel welcome. Someone else may have the gift of encouragement; therefore, they are looking for people they can minister to by praying with them. Perhaps their gift is exhortation and they are good at challenging others in love about their spiritual growth. There are many different gifts, talents and capabilities God enables us with and many Christians may have more than one.

Seek God through prayer and godly counsel asking Him to reveal your God given talents and capabilities. Once you have a good idea what your gifts are, then proceed to seek out your role and individual purpose within God's plan (which again will be through, by or for the local church). We all have a God given purpose which is part of God's ultimate plan that all come to repentance and that no one should perish. With the Bible as our guide and by fulfilling God's purpose for our lives within the structure of the new testament church, we will experience the peace that passeth all understanding.

I experienced this kind of peace only a few times in my life but look forward to experiencing this peace that passeth all understanding more and more. I keep asking God to "do it again" but what I am learning is that I need to get out of the way (and abandoned my agenda) and let God work though the purpose He has for my life.

I remember the first time I experienced the peace that passeth all understanding. You may think I am morbid, but it happened during my father's funeral. Back in 1966 when I was nine years old, my mother died of leukemia. I was devastated and cursed God. That was the beginning of my lack of regard for God and did not want anything to do with a God that would take away my mother. After pursing meaning for my life in all the wrong places and realizing that I needed God in my life I finally realized the true sacrificial love God has for me. When my Dad died in 1983, 4 years after I had accepted Jesus Christ as my savior, I was able to accept my Dad's death as His plan and thank Him for it. That day I experienced a wonderful peace from God, which overwhelmed me.

Another time I experienced this wonderful peace was the morning after climbing a mountain and hiking through the jungle to get to Adams in the Philippines on a missions trip. I woke very early and started my quiet time (time in prayer and reading the bible). The daily devotional I was using at the time was "My Utmost for His Highest" by Oswald Chambers. The devotion for that morning was titled "The Supreme Climb" referencing Abraham's obedience to God by taking his son Isaac on a hike up the mountain to offer Isaac on the alter as a sacrifice to God (Genesis 22:2-14). The emphasis of this devotion was that Abraham "rose up early" in obedience to God.

- "And Abraham rose up early in the morning, and saddled his ass, and took two of his young men with him, and Isaac his son, and clave the wood for the burnt offering, and rose up, and went unto the place of which God had told him." Genesis 22:3

He did not debate with God, nor did he question His authority. He immediately obeyed God. The principle taught is when God prompts us to do something we need to obey immediately. It was during the reading of that devotion I realized that God wanted me to be involved with missions and I surrendered with tears streaming down my face thanking Him for allowing a sinner like me to be a part of His great work. I experienced the peace that passeth all understanding and remember it as if it were yesterday.

My sincere desire is that you will seek out God's purpose for your life and not end up looking back on your life being unfulfilled because of what could have been. There will be no greater reward or return on our investment than fulfilling God's purpose in our lives. Eternal significance is the objective.

**Chapter 7, questions to ponder:**

1. Describe a time when you experienced peace that was beyond your understanding.

2. In what activities have you experienced the most peace?

3. Consider what God's purpose is for your life and how the activities of executing that purpose would deliver peace in your life.

4. Under whose authority do you think you would experience the most peace?

5. What are you doing to have an eternal significance in the lives of others?